WEIRD SPORTS

Brianna Kaiser

Lerner Publications ◆ Minneapolis

Lerner Publications Company
An imprint of Lerner Publishing Group, Inc.
241 First Avenue North
Minneapolis, MN 55401 USA

For reading levels and more information, look up this title at www.lernerbooks.com.

Main body text set in Aptifer Sans LT Pro.
Typeface provided by Linotype AG.

Editor: Lauren Foley **Designer:** Mary Ross

Library of Congress Cataloging-in-Publication Data

Names: Kaiser, Brianna, 1996– author.
Title: Weird sports / Brianna Kaiser.
Description: Minneapolis, MN : Lerner Publications, [2024] | Series: Wonderfully weird. Alternator books | Includes bibliographical references and index. | Audience: Ages 8–12 | Audience: Grades 4–6 | Summary: "People across the globe love to play sports. But not all sports are as common as others. Dash into the world of weird sports, including everyday activities taken to the extreme, combined sports, and more"— Provided by publisher.
Identifiers: LCCN 2022037017 (print) | LCCN 2022037018 (ebook) | ISBN 9781728490748 (library binding) | ISBN 9798765601952 (ebook)
Subjects: LCSH: Extreme sports—Juvenile literature.
Classification: LCC GV749.7 .K35 2024 (print) | LCC GV749.7 (ebook) | DDC 796.04/6—dc23/eng/20220825

LC record available at https://lccn.loc.gov/2022037017
LC ebook record available at https://lccn.loc.gov/2022037018

Manufactured in the United States of America
1-53005-51023-12/6/2022

TABLE OF CONTENTS

INTRODUCTION:

THE LARGEST DODGEBALL GAME

TWO TEAMS STAND ON OPPOSITE SIDES OF A GYM AND WAIT TO GRAB A BALL FROM THE CENTER. The gym teacher blows a whistle to start the game. Then everyone races to grab a ball and throw it at the opposing players. Someone hits an opponent with a ball, knocking them out of the game. This is dodgeball.

On September 25, 2012, in Irvine, California, over six thousand people set a Guinness World Record for the largest dodgeball game. Many types of sports exist. Some people take common sports to an extreme, such as playing a large dodgeball game. Some sports can seem odder than other sports. They can be weird! Sports can be weird in all kinds of ways.

CHAPTER 1:
PLAYING AT AN EXTREME

SOME PEOPLE TAKE SPORTS TO THE NEXT LEVEL.
They may also take everyday activities and objects and
make them extreme sports.

EXTREME IRONING

Ironing is usually done at home. But is that too boring? Extreme ironing is an adrenaline sport. People have ironed while rock climbing, scuba diving, and skydiving. The sport grew in popularity all over the world. Germany had the first Extreme Ironing World Championships in 2002. A documentary was even made in the United Kingdom about the sport.

Matthew Battley is an extreme ironer from New Zealand. He hiked to the top of Mount Ruapehu, an active volcano. The rocks on top of the volcano were hot enough that Battley could heat his iron on them. Battley has also ironed on lakes and in caves.

An extreme ironer competing in a forest

Rock Paper Scissors

The world's largest tournament of rock paper scissors took place in Tianjin Joy City, China. Over ten thousand people participated in the tournament on December 24, 2019.

ZORBING

In 1994 New Zealand's Andrew Akers and Dwane van der Sluis invented the zorb. The giant inflatable sphere is like a hamster exercise ball for humans. People go zorbing to roll down hills, ride for fun, and compete in races.

There are multiple Guinness World Records for zorbing. In 2006 in New Zealand, Steve Camp traveled the longest single-roll distance ever in a zorb. He went about 1,870 feet (570 m). James Duggan has the fastest 100-meter zorbing time at 23.21 seconds. He set the record in 2019 in Ireland.

Kids play in zorbs.

YUKIGASSEN

The sport Yukigassen, or snow battle, started in Japan in 1989. International Alliance of Yukigassen formed in 2013 to promote the growth of the sport worldwide.

Two teams of seven players take their positions on opposite sides of a court. Yukigassen sets last for three minutes, and the team that wins two sets first is the winner. The teams begin each set with ninety snowballs. If a person is hit by a snowball, they are out. To win the set, one team has to eliminate more opponents than the other team. They can also win the set by capturing the flag from the opposing team's side of the court.

A Yukigassen event in Norway

WHAT ARE SPORTS?

People disagree about what they consider a sport. Many say sports are exclusively physical activities where people compete against one another, such as volleyball and soccer. But esports, or electronic sports, are video game competitions. The esports industry is worth over $1 billion! Many people consider activities like chess to be sports too. Chess is a mind sport. Players compete with mental strength instead of physical ability.

CHAPTER 2:
PLAYING UNDERWATER

MANY SPORTS TAKE PLACE UNDERWATER. Whether they are a unique sport or a version of another sport, these games draw people in from all over the globe.

BOG SNORKELLING

The World Bog Snorkelling Championships have occurred every year in Wales since 1985. Competitors come from all around the world. They wear a snorkel and flippers as they swim through a bog. The bog, a freshwater wetland, has a trench path the swimmers follow. The path is about 196 feet (60 m) long.

Neil Rutter holds the record for the fastest swim through the trench at the World Bog Snorkelling Championships. The art teacher from the United Kingdom has won the event three times.

Bog snorkellers sometimes wear other gear like swim caps.

Two teams fighting for the ball during an underwater rugby match

UNDERWATER RUGBY

In rugby, players throw or kick an oval ball. The sport has elements of American football and soccer. Imagine playing rugby underwater. Two teams compete and try to score points by placing the ball into the opponent's basket. The baskets are at the bottom of each end of the pool.

Underwater rugby started in Cologne, Germany, in the 1960s. Underwater rugby teams are in the US, Colombia, Hungary, Australia, and other countries. In 2014 an underwater rugby club, the First Asian Team Underwater Rugby, formed in Singapore. They hope to grow the sport in Asia.

Underwater hockey players move the puck with short pusher sticks.

UNDERWATER HOCKEY

People play underwater hockey in a pool that is 6 to 13 feet (2 to 4 m) deep. Two teams of six players wear snorkels and flippers and use small pusher sticks. It is a noncontact sport, so players should not pull or grab one another.

Using their pusher sticks, the players move a weighted puck along the bottom of a pool toward their opponent's goal. Unlike ice or field hockey, no goalies play in underwater hockey. Instead, teams work together in formations to defend their goals. The goals are about 9 feet (3 m) wide. Each game has two halves that are fifteen minutes long.

Swim Fin Hurdles

When people compete in hurdles, a track-and-field event, they usually don't wear swim fins. In 2008 Germany's Christopher Irmscher set a record for fastest 100-meter hurdles while wearing swim fins.

CHAPTER 3:

SPORTS WITH A TWIST

SOME SPORTS HAVE A WEIRD TWIST. Each of these sports features a unique or unexpected element.

A dog and owner surf together in the 2021 Surf City Surf Dog event in California.

DOG SURFING

Dog surfing is just what it sounds like. Since the 1920s in California and Hawaii, dogs have surfed in competitions. Judges score the dogs by their skills on the boards, how long they are on the boards, and the sizes of the waves. The dog with the highest score wins the event. In some events, dogs surf with a person. In other events, the dogs surf alone.

In 2011 the dog Abbie Girl set the record for longest wave surfed by a dog. Abbie Girl surfed 351.7 feet (107.2 m) in San Diego, California.

Basketball and Surfing

On August 31, 2013, Bernie Boehm of the US spun a basketball while surfing for 33.25 seconds. The feat earned him a Guinness World Record.

SEPAK TAKRAW

Also known as kick volleyball, Sepak Takraw is played in many countries such as Malaysia, Thailand, the Philippines, Pakistan, and the US. It is similar to volleyball, but players don't use their hands. They hit the ball with their feet, knees, chests, and heads.

The game is played with three members on each team, or regus. One player, the tekong, stays in the back. The tekong serves the ball to begin play. Then each player on the team can only touch the ball once before hitting it over the net. The game has three sets, each played to 21 points. The team that wins two sets wins the game.

Sepak Takraw players
have to leap or twist t
without their h

THE OLYMPICS

Over two hundred countries participate in the Summer and Winter Olympic Games. The Olympics began around three thousand years ago with sports such as boxing and chariot racing. In its long history, the Olympics has included some odd sports, including tug-of-war! Tug-of-war was part of five Olympic Games from 1900 to 1920.

BOSSABALL

During trips to Brazil in the 1990s, Filip Eyckmans of Belgium was inspired by capoeira. Capoeira is a Brazilian martial art that combines dance, music, and acrobatics. In the early 2000s, Eyckmans created bossaball. The sport is a new kind of volleyball that combines elements of multiple sports, including capoeira and soccer.

People play bossaball on an inflatable court that has a trampoline on each side of the net. Teams have four players who can hit the ball with any part of their bodies. Each team is only allowed to touch the ball five times before returning it over the net.

A bossaball player leaping to hit the ball

CHAPTER 4:

SPORTS WITH FOOD?

HAVE YOU EVER LEARNED ABOUT SPORTS THAT INVOLVE FOOD? They are more common than you might think! Some sports are centered on food, but not for eating.

CHEESE ROLLING

Each year, people from all over the world head to Gloucester, England, to compete in the Cooper's Hill Cheese Roll. Competitors chase a Double Gloucester cheese wheel down Cooper's Hill, which is about 200 yards (183 m) long.

The cheese wheel can go up to 70 miles (113 km) per hour downhill. The person who makes it down the hill first wins. And they get to keep the cheese!

No one knows when the race first started. A written account of the event says it took place in 1826. But many believe it started long before then.

Abby Lampe (*left*) celebrates her 2022 women's cheese rolling race win with the 2021 winner.

Many people gather to watch the West Coast Giant Pumpkin Regatta.

PUMPKIN RACING

In October many people carve pumpkins for Halloween or for fun. But some people find huge pumpkins, carve them, and ride in them like boats. They even race them in the West Coast Giant Pumpkin Regatta in Oregon. The pumpkins used in the race can weigh over 1,500 pounds (680 kg).

Some people go to Oregon just to watch the races. But people enjoy other pumpkin-related activities during the race and festival, including pumpkin bowling and pumpkin golf.

A family paddling in a milk carton boat race in Minnesota

MILK CARTON REGATTA

There are many boat races around the world. For some races, the boats have to be made out of milk cartons. The Masters Milk Carton Regatta takes place near Perth, Australia. People compete in the race with family and friends for prize money. Other milk carton boat races take place all around the world including in the US and Latvia.

Foods on the Run

Some people run marathons in costumes that make them look like foods such as hot dogs. Jordan Maddocks of the US has Guinness World Records for fastest marathon times dressed as a vegetable and a fruit.

MORE WEIRD SPORTS

People play many weird sports, and it is not possible to include them all in this book. And some people may define *weird* or *sports* in different ways. What do you think is a weird sport? Do your friends agree or disagree? Which weird sport is your favorite?

Pumpkin bowling is another fun and unusual fall sport.

GLOSSARY

acrobatics: an act of balance and agility

adrenaline: a hormone your body releases in response to a stress or threat, such as extreme heights

competition: a contest or game people try to win

formation: a way a team arranges themselves

inflatable: able to make larger or expand

martial art: a combat skill

regatta: a boat race or series of boat races

set: a round of a competition or sport

snorkel: a tube used by a swimmer for breathing with their head underwater

trench: a deep, narrow ditch

LEARN MORE

Berne, Emma Carlson. *The World of Adventure Sports*. Oakland, CA: Lonely Planet Global Limited, 2020.

Britannica Kids: Sports
https://kids.britannica.com/kids/article/sports/390852

Gifford, Clive. *Sports: Facts at Your Fingertips*. New York: DK Children, 2021.

Kenney, Karen Latchana. *Extreme Endurance Challenges*. Minneapolis: Lerner Publications, 2021.

Scheff, Matt. *The Summer Olympics: World's Best Athletic Competition*. Minneapolis: Lerner Publications, 2021.

Sport Facts for Kids
https://kids.kiddle.co/Sport

Sports Illustrated Kids: More Sports
https://www.sikids.com/more-sports

Weird but True! Sports
https://kids.nationalgeographic.com/weird-but-true/article/sports

INDEX

PHOTO ACKNOWLEDGMENTS

Image credits: Jae C. Hong/AP Images, pp. 4, 5; The Asahi Shimbun/Getty Images, pp. 6, 7; Johnny Green/PA Images/Getty Images, p. 7; DBenitostock/Getty Images, p. 8; Kristian Buus/In Pictures/Getty Images Images, p. 9; Samuel Bay/Alamy Stock Photo, p. 10; David Jones/PA Images/Getty Images, p. 12; Fotograferen.net/Alamy Stock Photo, p. 13; LUIS ROBAYO/AFP/Getty Images, pp. 14, 15; MOHD RASFAN/AFP/Getty Images, p. 16; Jasmin Merdan/Getty Images, p. 17; Rouelle Umali/Xinhua/Getty Images, p. 18; Mindy Schauer/Digital First Media/Orange County Register/Getty Images, p. 19; NHAC NGUYEN/AFP/Getty Images, p. 20; Jaap Arriens/Alamy Stock Photo, pp. 22, 23; Cameron Smith/Getty Images, pp. 24, 25; Italarico/Shutterstock, pp. 26,27; Marlin Levison/Star Tribune/Getty Images, p. 28; Michael Wheatley/Alamy Stock Photo, p. 29.

Cover: Tony Andrews /EyeEm/Getty Images.